LAUGH
the D

SHORT STORIES WITH A SHIVER

Contents

Laughing in the Dark 2
Babysitting .25
Waiting to be Collected 41
Badger 56

Written by June Evans
Illustrated by Rhiannon Powell

Collins Educational
An imprint of HarperCollinsPublishers

Laughing in the Dark

We were all supposed to feel sorry for Auntie May, though she didn't seem to need it.

"You're not to say a word about Uncle Michael, mind. Not a word, you hear me, you two?" My mother was folding the tablecloth, smoothing its starched surface before putting it away in the sideboard drawer.

"Why, what's he done?" My sister asked such questions automatically. She always had more to say than I did, but, all the same, she was not really interested. Like my mother and all the aunts, she kept talking as if it was important to fill up the spaces in the day with chatter.

The house always seemed full of women in those days, women in aprons gathered in the kitchen, talking and laughing together. Of course, they were not really aunts, just friends who lived nearby, but the title was a politeness my mother insisted on. When I was a boy they would be in and out of each other's houses all day long, till dusk fell and the men came home from work. Our back door was never locked and, in summer, when the weather allowed, it stayed wide open all day long.

"He's just gone off, that's what. The silly creature. He doesn't know when he's well off. After all your Auntie May's done for him, too. Now, not a word. I don't know how May ever put up with..." She stopped and gave us a long considering look, then carried on as if she couldn't help herself. " A weak excuse for a man if ever I saw one and lazy as a stuffed cushion." Mary giggled and mother tutted and shook her head.

The room was full of damp air which rose, warm and gentle, from the wooden clotheshorse placed on three sides around the open fire and also drifted in from the racks of washing hung high to dry under the ceiling in the scullery. It was a Monday and Mother was pink with exertion and pride at a job well done. There were no washing machines or driers in ordinary folk's homes in those days and it was a long day's labour with cold leftovers to eat and keep out of mother's way till the job was done.

"Where's he gone? London?" I really wanted to know. London was a magical name for a faraway place, like Timbuctoo or Zanzibar. My friend Stanley had a friend who lived near London and who had been taken to the Festival of Britain.

I was much more curious about people and places than Mary but my questions usually went unanswered. I remember I found it hard to be taken seriously at home as I was the only boy. I had two older sisters apart from Mary; one was married and the other, Polly, had gone away to be a nurse.

Occasionally, on days off, Polly would catch a bus home and have tea with us and tell stories of sawn-off legs and stitched stomachs till my mother, becoming squeamish, told her to stop it or else.

I suppose I was petted and made much of; certainly Mary always complained that I was. The aunts used to give me gingerbread and big peppermints that bulged my mouth; occasionally even their sweet ration coupons so that I had to beg the money from Mum in order to go and spend them. They patted my head and said what a mercy it was that the war was over, then forgot me as they talked around the fireplace, sipping from cups of strong tea.

Sometimes, as a treat, I was allowed to assemble my Meccano on a tray in the neat, polished, smaller front room. I could hear their voices still, soothingly rising and falling.

Auntie May lived in the end house of the row, the one with the big garden. You could walk right round May's house on the far side so you didn't have to go through the house to get to the back garden. Not that anyone much came to the front doors except the insurance man who called each week to collect a shilling and write in the grey book which was kept, in our house, in the drawer of the sideboard in the front room. Everybody else came along the lane at the back and in at the back door; the men came home this way from work and the children from school.

May was the jolliest of the neighbours. She was shaped like a cottage loaf, with a round, red and white smiling face set on top of a rounder body which was pulled in halfway down. Her face was creased with laughing and her eyes shone; her hair was frizzy and the colour of new conkers and billowed around her head. People said she was a handsome woman. The idea of May being sad was hard to imagine and when I peered at her through the fringe of black hair, which my mother was always sweeping away from my forehead, or wanting to cut, she seemed the same as ever. I was glad for I liked May and she was surely the best baker of cakes and bread in the whole town;

there was usually something tasty for me in the pocket of her flowered apron.

"Come on in, May," my mother called that same day, "I'm just about to put the kettle on," and, with a warning look at us, she lifted the big black kettle and carried it to the stone sink. Mary took this as permission to leave but I still hovered there trying to look inconspicuous. I am, still, curious about people and I was also a greedy little boy.

"Sit down, take the weight off your feet. Have you heard anything?"

Mother ushered the visitor through the steam of the scullery and into the large, cosy kitchen where we spent most of our time. She moved the drying clothes to one side of the fire and May sat in the rocking chair. She didn't look sad, she looked determined.

"Not a word, just cleared off and left everything except the clothes he stood up in."

"Ah, I'm sorry, May." Mother took the teapot into the scullery.

"You needn't be," May called after her. "He walked in from nowhere six years ago, just back from the war and no family to go to, or so he said, and now he's walked out again."

"Ah, but you must find it hard and it's not as if it's the first ti..." My mother stopped there as if she'd made a mistake about what she was going to say. She seemed flustered. "Help yourself to sugar." She pushed the basin towards the other woman.

"Well, I'm not going to spend time moping. There's other things to think of."

"That's the way," my mother said cheeringly. May nodded and rocked in the chair. Her eyes twinkled at me and out of her pocket she brought a fairy cake with white icing on top, wrapped in a bit of rustling greaseproof paper. She held it out to me and laughed uproariously as I took it, as if it was the greatest joke in the world. I walked into the back garden to eat it. I considered her to be very brave indeed.

May put up a notice in her front room the following week. It had a neat, red, ruled border and, in best handwriting, it announced: Vacancy - Room to let. Suit single gentleman.

I wondered if that was how Uncle Mike had arrived

in the first place but decided not to ask. It was the sort of question that grown-ups would be sure to consider cheeky.

The Auntie May Business, as my mother called it, got a good airing the following weekend. Sunday was a day for family, not neighbours, and Grandad had come as usual for his dinner. Mostly he cycled the three miles from the village where he had lived all his life, but that day he had been brought by car. He was wearing his best suit, kept for Sundays and funerals, and he sat in the rocking chair with his elbows on the wooden arms and took wispy, brown and gold, stringy tobacco from a tin and placed it along the middle of an oblong of thin paper. When he had arranged it evenly and to his satisfaction, he licked one edge of the paper and rolled and stuck it. Grandad never used the ashtray that Mum put in the hearth for him but always leaned forward to shake the ash into the fire. Sometimes he left it too late and then grey flakes would spatter his Sunday-best trousers and he would brush at them and catch my eye and wink.

Often he would cough, not a polite little sound like the aunts made, but great racking gusts. My mother always said Grandad smoked too much and his lungs must be in a terrible way and she would look meaningfully at Dad when she said it. She never actually complained to Grandad, just tutted and pursed up her mouth and bustled away to do something.

"It's not the cigarettes," he always told me, "don't you believe them. It's the coal dust, my lungs are full of it."

Uncle Percy and Aunt Vi were there that Sunday. Aunt Vi was Dad's sister, thin and dark and prickly. They had two children but only Pamela had come with them. I wasn't sorry; William, my other cousin, was two years older than me and the last time he had visited he'd sat on the front garden wall and whistled at the girls going past. He'd call out things like, "Hi, goodlooking," and "What's cooking?" I was so embarrassed I had to crouch down behind the wall and pretend to be looking for something in the grass.

This Sunday afternoon, Mary and Pamela went off together to the park. The grown-ups moved into the chilly front room and sat uncomfortably on the almost new chairs sipping tiny glasses of port wine. Grandad was restless; Mum didn't allow smoking in the front room. I sat at the table in the bay window and listened to them while keeping my eyes on the road outside.

"... always a bit shiftless, Mike. Lazy, you know. May used to wait on him hand and foot. He wouldn't have suited me, that's for sure."

"Poor devil," Grandad muttered.

"Now then, Pa, he didn't know when he was well off. The trouble she took over him. He would have lost his job more than once if May hadn't gone and spoken up for him. Then to walk out without a word like that."

"P'raps he woke up and realised what a busybody he'd got himself stuck with. More than just a busybody too, I shouldn't wonder," Grandad retorted.

"Oh, whatever do you mean?" Aunt Vi had a thin, shrill voice to match her bird-like ways.

"Well, that woman, May... got the evil eye she has, that one. I've come across it before."

There was a shocked silence, followed by feminine laughter.

"Get away with you, you're a wicked old man."

"Evil eye indeed!"

"What's that then? Something from your village past? Don't tell me they're still burning witches," Dad was laughing now.

Grandad stuck out his chin. "Well, then, it was from the village, and no laughing matter either."

"A witch d'you mean? Come on, tell us the tale, we can't promise to believe it but we'll try." Vi looked round for approval and again shrieked with laughter.

Grandad looked disapproving. "You may laugh, 'tis not so funny for all that." He patted the pocket where his tobacco was. "We had a woman lived just outside the village, just like your May she was, good-looking woman, too. But for all that she had the evil eye; known for it, she was. We were warned to keep away from her when we were childer. We daren't cross such a one."

My mother looked uncomfortable. "What nonsense you talk, Pa. You hardly know May. What a thing to say, evil eye indeed."

"I don't need to know her, I can tell."

"What did she do, with her eye?" I burst out.

"Now you see what you've started," Mother grumbled. "A load of old gossip and nonsense."

"I need a fag," was all the answer she got.

"Into the kitchen then," Mum said and, after he'd shambled away, "I wouldn't put it past him to have started all that nonsense just so that I'd be glad to see the back of him. He's been dying for a cigarette." She laughed, "Cunning old so-and-so. Evil eye indeed!"

"Whatever did she see in this Mike, then?" Vi returned to the previous topic of conversation.

"Oh, I don't know. She said he made her laugh. Always one for a good laugh, May is. He was a bit of a joker, I suppose. She set great store by a sense of humour."

"Reckon he's gone off to London?"

"That's mostly where they seem to go, or maybe Bristol, it's nearer."

"P'raps he'll be back when the money runs out."

"He didn't have much, May says. She seems to think he's gone for good."

"Ah, I expect there's more than she's telling." Vi nodded her head as if she knew everything about such behaviour. "Very likely they had a row and she doesn't like to say so."

I slipped away to join Grandad. He was pinching strands of tobacco between a finger and thumb.

"What's the evil eye, Grandad?"

He went on with what he was doing and seemed not to have heard. When he had pressed the paper edges together he fixed his faded eyes on my face and sighed. "Just old stories," he said and put the paper tube into his mouth.

"Didn't you really know anyone with it, then?" I let him see what a disappointment he was to me.

"Well," he drew on the glowing tobacco and seemed to relax. "I wouldn't say that exactly. There was an old woman… people took care not to cross her."

I wouldn't let him off that easily. "Why? What did she do?" I knew from history lessons that people had believed in witches and devils and things. He seemed to wish he hadn't said anything about it. I persisted. "Tell me what sort of things she did. Did she put spells on people?"

"They said she could stop hens from laying, stop cows from giving milk, put a blight on crops, that sort of thing. That was very serious for people. The villagers would put little gifts on her doorstep to keep in her good books."

"Go on! I'll bet she was just a poor old woman, probably had a black cat. I'll bet you used to call her names and then run away when you were a boy."

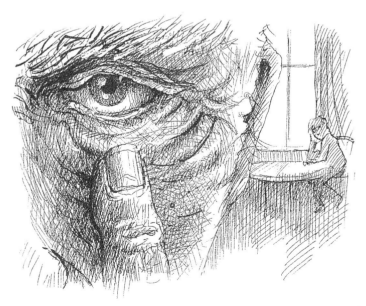

"Aye, we'd call her names, throw things, too, sometimes. We threw scrubby little apples at her door, not at her... we were too scared to do that. She'd look at you..." he stopped and picked a shred of tobacco off his lower lip, "and you'd feel you were shrivelling up inside, shrinking."

He seemed quite serious. "There was one boy who disappeared..." He came to a stop.

"What d'you mean, disappeared?"

"It was a mystery. They said later that he'd run away to join the army but... he was never seen or heard of again."

"What a load of old rubbish," I chortled. "Anyway, May isn't a bit like that, she's all laughing and nice. Her eyes are crinkled up with laughing."

"Aye, I expect you're right. I'm just getting old and imagining things." He stared into the fire.

I gazed at him with a cold touch of fear. What he said about getting old worried me. It was something I didn't want to think about. I didn't want Grandad to get older and then die.

"You're just a bit daft, Grandad, that's what." I punched him lightly on the arm to show that I knew he was still strong.

"Now then, saucy," he leaned over, dripped ash on his waistcoat, aimed a jabbing forefinger at my chest. "All the same," he said, "I'd keep away from that one, laddy, she's got the look."

It was several weeks before Auntie May found another lodger. The other aunts were divided about whether Uncle Mike would return or not.

"You'll see, he'll be back when he comes to his senses."

"Well, I hope he doesn't come back," put in one, younger than the rest.

"She's better off without him, if you ask me." This was greeted with frowns and shaken heads. "Mike was all right," was the general opinion.

Mike was a quiet man, or so he had seemed to me, though I didn't see him often. He was big, shambling awkwardly on huge feet, and, like a bear, he moved his head from side to side when he looked at you. Mostly when I saw him he was hidden behind a newspaper. He was clumsy, May said, always knocking things over, but she laughed as she said it. He usually had one or two bits of cottonwool sticking to his chin, where he had cut himself, so he must have been clumsy when he shaved, too. I was fascinated by the idea of shaving and longed to try it. Sometimes my father let me watch him shaving, the razor rasping as it left clear paths of skin through the piled snow of lather. If Dad was feeling playful he would dab the loaded brush at my face till I had a beard like Father Christmas. My father joked a lot but Mike was so silent I couldn't imagine him behaving like that. How could it be that May said he made her laugh when he hardly ever seemed to speak?

Whenever I had to go to May's on an errand, Mike would be sitting in the kitchen with his enormous feet in well-darned socks propped up on the shining brass fender that surrounded the fireplace. Unlike most of the houses where there would be a new gas cooker in the scullery and a proper tiled grate in the

kitchen, May had a huge black kitchen range with a fire built up behind bars and a large oven at one side with a thick, heavy iron door and great hinges and brass knobs. A big black kettle sat pouting on a hob above. It was always hot in May's kitchen. Twice a week the smell of hot new-baked bread escaped and spread along the street, tingling the noses of passers-by and filling them with longing.

May was famous for her baking. At Harvest Festival she baked a special loaf like a sheaf of corn for the church – not that she was a churchgoer herself. She was so clever that the corn looked alive and she would include a single poppy and sometimes a harvest mouse nibbling at a stalk.

On her mantelpiece, high above the shiny polished black range, there were other things that she baked – plaques like cottages with curtains and smoke curling from chimneys, bunches of flowers, a windmill, animals, all made out of dough, baked hard and painted.

I liked the animals best of all. There was one, a black and white cat so lifelike that I expected to see its tail swishing. I often told May that it was my favourite, hinting, you know, the way children do, that I would like to own it. She ignored all my efforts and later, when I discovered on that terrible day what she kept hidden away, I was very glad that I had nothing which May had made.

That fateful day, just a week before term was to begin and I was to become a new boy at the secondary school, the oven had been hard at work all day. There were loaves of all shapes and sizes piled on wire racks, spread over the big pale, scrubbed, wooden table, and if there is scent in heaven I think it must include the smell of new-baked bread.

"Here, take this to your mother, eat it while it's still fresh," May smiled and laughed at my drooling eyes and mouth.

Her face was red with the heat and the effort of stooping to the oven, her hair was tamed by perspiration to lie close to her forehead and ears. She wrapped a crusty loaf in a clean teacloth and thrust its warmth into my waiting arms.

"Tell her I've a gentleman coming on Saturday, name of Mr Donkins and all alone in the world, poor soul." She laughed again, "We'll have to see if we can cheer him up a bit, won't we?"

Later I was sent back to return the teacloth. May was not in the kitchen when I walked in and there was no answer when I called out. The bread had been put away in deep earthenware crocks in the cool scullery. I stopped on my way back to look at the black and white cat and then, on impulse, pulled a wooden chair close to stand on for a better look. It gazed malevolently at me. It was not, on closer inspection, a sweet, purring rub-around-the-legs sort of cat but a fierce-eyed animal about to spit at a hated enemy. If I had been younger I think it would have frightened me. Instead, I felt challenged by its open hostility and wondered why May had made it like that.

There was a key at the edge of the shelf, right next to a closed cupboard which was built into the space beside the fireplace. I picked it up and idly wondered if it fitted the cupboard lock. I have already said that I was curious about people; I was the sort of child who looked in the pockets of coats and in dressing-table drawers, and it occurred to me that I had never seen that cupboard open.

The kettle was hissing on the range, emphasising the silence of the house. There were no footsteps outside. Perhaps it was the stillness that invited me to search for secrets. I had never come across anything hidden that was shameful or frightening and never expected to. If I had even dreamed of such things I would never have slipped that key in the lock and opened that cupboard door.

Almost before I could think of it, I had done it. The door swung wide and I almost fell off the chair with shock.

I was face to face with Uncle Mike. A small, neat, replica of the man stood on a shelf confronting me. It was so lifelike, so weird, that for a moment it took my breath away in a gasp. Then I realised what it was and gasped again with admiration. He was perfect in every detail. Auntie May had captured his wiry hair and his red-veined nose, his bulky, untidy shape and large bear's feet. The wrinkles and bagging at the knees of his trousers, the dust around his shoes, frayed laces, the hairs on the backs of his hands and sprouting from inside the dark caverns of his nose were all there. There were even – I gazed enraptured – two tiny pieces of cotton wool under his right ear with a dull red patch at the centre of each. He looked exactly as I had seen him last.

I began to feel uneasy; it crept up on me slowly, the unhappy awareness that this was something more than a painted, dough figurine. You see, I had seen and spoken to Uncle Mike on the evening before he disappeared. I had been playing in the lane and Mike came past as usual, wheeling his bicycle, on his way home. He tripped as he approached me and caught the end of his trouser leg on the swinging pedal. I remember the sound of tearing cloth and the swear word he muttered.

"Now what'll I do?" He looked ridiculously dismayed.

"What's the matter?" I went up to him and

surveyed the damage. "Auntie May will soon mend that, won't she?"

"Hmm. I'm in her bad books already today. Let's hope she doesn't notice till tomorrow, eh? Maybe she'll be feeling better by then."

I thought this very strange. I had never seen May when she was not cheerful, full of bubbling laughter. I just couldn't imagine her cross. Still, grown-ups had moods, I knew that, and were often quite different when they were with other adults and didn't know they were being watched.

I fished in my trouser pocket and lifted out a handful of small objects, certain that I had put a safetypin there a few days before. I brushed the fluff away and handed it to him.

"Thanks, that might do the trick." He bent to fasten the torn cloth while I held his bicycle.

"Not too bad," I commented. He had pinned it tidily on the inside so that only the merest speck of silver metal showed and the tear was hidden.

That had happened over three weeks ago and nobody, as far as I knew, except Auntie May of course, had ever seen Mike again. For some reason this floated up in my mind and a cold finger seemed to trace my spine right up to my hair. I felt that I knew something but I hadn't even worked out what exactly it was – and I didn't want to.

I looked further into the cupboard to keep my eyes away from the figure of Mike and, further back on the same shelf were two other figures – both men, both looking at me with dismayed and fearful eyes. That sentence that my mother had never quite finished

came into my mind: "It isn't as if it's the first ti..." She had stopped herself but the word 'time' was clear as a bell – not the first time. Not the first time that a man had disappeared.

With shaking hands I lifted the figure of Mike from the shelf and examined the left trouser leg. There was the tiny glint of silver – the safetypin I had lent him, and there was a thread of torn cloth. I stared into his face and his eyes looked back at me, mournful, pleading. I felt that I was holding something strange and terrifying; something alive. My hands shook and I tried to still the half-thoughts that tumbled in my mind and surfaced as sheer terror. I had to use both hands as I placed the statue back onto the shelf and closed the door. As I did so I felt the eyes of all three mannikins fixed on me as if begging for something – something I could not give them. Turning the key in the door I knew that I was confining them again to a dark prison, or worse.

How I managed to replace the key, step down and move the chair, I do not know, but it was desperately important that May did not find out I had been spying, or what might my own fate be? I crept from the house and slipped along the lane to the safety of home. Once there, I flung myself face down onto the bed and shivered with dread. My grandfather's warning kept repeating itself in my brain.

That was a long time ago and the next day, and many times after, I wondered if I had been dreaming. One thing was sure, I didn't intend to put it to the test. I did see Uncle Mike once again as it happens, and even now thinking of it makes my flesh cringe.

It was the following week, Friday I think, and I was coming home alone across the waste ground at the end of our street. Grass and weeds were slowly taking over the site where the biscuit factory used to stand before the Germans bombed it. The ground was still uneven with lumps of rubble; it was dusk and, knowing I was later than my mother expected me to be, I was hurrying. My right foot slid sideways into a hole with my weight behind it and I cried out with the sudden jolt and pain. After a few minutes the worst of the agony had died away leaving an ache which I thought I could cope with. I soon discovered that trying to put any weight on the ankle brought back an instant stabbing and I hobbled and hopped as best I could to the end house – May's.

It would be quicker to go through her garden.

The front of the house was unlit, as was to be expected, but there was no light spilling from the side window either. I had no intention of meeting May, in fact, though I now felt I had probably over-reacted when I saw the figures and imagined far too much, I was scared of having to see or speak to her again. So, I skirted the side of the house cautiously. Flickers of light, I now realised, were coming from the fire in the kitchen but that was all. It seemed that May was out and I crept nearer. In between the occasional glimmers all was dark and silent.

Then I heard it. The sound burst from the house and caught me like an unexpected blow so that I sank to my knees, whimpering, while icy fingers shrank the hairs on my head and neck. The noise was all around me in the darkness, horrible, inhuman. It was the sound of glee, malicious, vile.

I have never heard laughter like that before or since. It filled the night and invaded my head. It was the laughter of a madman – or rather woman – for I realised at once who was doing the laughing.

I was stuck there on my hands and knees below the kitchen window, rigid, unable to move for what seemed ages. When I had recovered a little I raised myself up. The noise had stopped and I knew I had to look inside – I had to see what May was doing, what had caused her to laugh so uproariously, so horribly in the lonely darkness of her house.

She was sitting in one of her two fireside chairs. The flickering flames illuminated the side of her face and one plump arm which rested on the side of the chair. As I peered in she laughed again; she shook with the depth and strength of her hilarity. Her mouth must have been wide open to let forth such gales which surely came from deep inside her. From time to time she would moan and pause and her other hand then came up to wipe her eyes.

It filled me with horror. It was so reckless, so unheeding, so callous and unnatural. It interrupted the night and tore it apart. I was surprised that people didn't come running. It seemed as if she would never stop. I wanted to cover up her head, to stuff something into that mouth, anything to bring that dreadful noise to a halt. Then I saw where her gaze was directed; my own eyes followed and stretched wide.

The cupboard door was open. Exposed to view in the dim, inconstant light were the three little male figures, like dolls all in a row.

For a few seconds she went quiet and I shrank again below the window frame, even more terrified of discovery. Then the huge gusts of merriment started up again, like bitter vengeful waves that flung themselves against the unfeeling models. At least I hope they were unfeeling and unseeing but they were so lifelike that it seemed they might move at any moment.

I ducked away and, moving as fast as I could, reached home and my bed, hardly noticing the pain of my twisted ankle.

I only ever saw May in the distance after that. I took care to avoid her and it is with a shudder that I think of her, even now, all these years later.

My mother became ill that year and the following year Grandad died. We moved into his cottage in the country, believing the country air would benefit Mum, and I have never been back to that street where we lived. It is all a very long time ago but if ever I hear unrestrained laughter, my hands clench and I break into a sweat. The horror of it will always be with me; the sound of it still rings in my ears on bad nights when I lie awake. I can still hear that laughing, laughing, laughing in the dark.

Babysitting

"Jumble sales," Francie mumbled through her biscuit. Everybody groaned. Even she did not bother to look enthusiastic about the idea, or hurt at the response.

"Sponsored silence?" Katy offered more hopefully. "Parents usually go for that."

"Cake sale, shoe cleaning, car wash," Melanie was despondent.

Francie was shaking her head. "They get fed up with the same things all the time."

"Yeah, mine say, 'Not again, it's sheer blackmail'." Penny pulled a face, losing her eyes somewhere under her eyebrows as she mimed adult exasperation.

"That's an idea," Katy put in, stretching her arms as if she had just woken up.

"What?"

"Blackmail." They all stared.

"Blackmail who?" Penny asked, acknowledging possibilities.

Katy cast her mind over her friends and relations, considering them in the light of possible victims. Who among them looked like the possessor of a shameful, possibly sinister, secret?

"Our next-door neighbours look a bit weird," she said.

It wasn't so much the adults who looked peculiar as the child, or rather, it was the fact that they didn't seem to belong together that was odd. Katy tried to explain this to the others but they only laughed.

"Are you trying to tell us that they're kidnappers?" Penny alone seemed intrigued. "People do take babies, sometimes, if they can't have any of their own," she added.

"Huh, they can have my brother any time," Francie told them. "They'd have to be mad to want him."

"How could we find out? And would they pay us money not to tell?" Penny was getting quite interested in the idea. "Should we spy on them, follow them about?"

"Depends," was all Katy would reply.

"Great grimacing gargoyles! You lot are as cracked as empty eggshells. I just don't believe what I'm hearing." Francie pushed her wiry black hair away from her forehead in an exasperated manner.

Nobody quailed or quivered and not a single eyelash was batted. They were used to Francie's expressions of disgust and indignation and this one was at least a week old. "If you did discover something like that, you'd have to go to the police," she went on knowingly.

"I'm not saying they're kidnappers," Katy protested, " 'course I'm not. It's just they're kind of odd."

Everybody relaxed, though with a feeling of disappointment. The possibility of undertaking a criminal, possibly dangerous, activity had hung tantalisingly in all their minds for a few astonishing moments. Now it faded and they laughed at each other, and Francie threw the last crumbs of biscuit at Katy before screwing up the empty packet and casting it into the brambles.

The dip in the ground behind Francie's father's garden shed was just the right size for sheltering the four of them, allowing them to huddle within the surrounding tangle where he did not bother to exercise his gardening skills. Two planks served as a drawbridge to cross the prickly barrier and also as seats. They were, once seated, effectively screened from all but the very tall.

"What about babysitting?" Katy's mother suggested. "The new couple next door might be needing someone."

"I've never sat on a baby yet," Katy retorted, "and I'm not sure that I want to, even for cash."

"Well, I don't suppose he bites. You might as well give it a go. You never know, you might like it and if you're just next door, I could be round in a minute if you needed help."

"Why should I need help?" She spoke indignantly, "I'm not stupid or anything."

"Hmmm."

"Anyway, have they asked?"

"It has been mentioned as a possibility, no more."

"Well, I dunno."

"I'm a bit early I know, only Mum thought it would be a good idea for the baby to sort of get used to me, so he won't be frightened if he wakes up," Katy explained. She was still wondering how she had been persuaded to do this.

The man beamed at her and led her into the kitchen-diner. He was tall and thin with dark brown, melancholy eyes of the kind that animals often have and which are described as liquid or appealing, or both. His hair, Katy noticed, grew into a point at the back of his head and rested like an arrow pointing down his back. He had thin arms and shoulders and the arms and hands hung loosely as if they should have been occupied with doing something and were surprised to find themselves empty.

"Here's, er, um, Katy," he told his wife. "She's, er, come early, to inspect our little, um, monster," and he laughed so that his shoulders shook and the long thin arms and fine-boned hands swung gently.

Mrs Bamber sat at the round table, a spoon held in mid-air before her child's face. "Open wide," she intoned, glancing only briefly at Katy, her attention concentrated on the baby as if she was taking part in work of enormous importance. "And again," she scooped at the food, "open up big, big, mouth, grroarr." She smiled and opened her own mouth and the child did likewise, making a similar roaring sound and seizing the spoon in his jaws. He shook it from side to side, "Grrr, grrr, grrr."

The woman laughed and clapped her hands. "Isn't he a clever boy? He's a little king, he is. What a strong boy. Now, last one, let Mummy have the spoon, let it go…" She tugged and the child relinquished it with a throaty gurgle.

"What strong toothypegs he's got. Now, one last spoonful to make Leo a big strong boy." She scraped around the dish and thrust a last offering of reddish meat and gravy forward. "Yummy, yumm," she cried, "eat it all up."

Positively sick-making, was Katy's unspoken verdict, looking from one to the other of the doting parents. They were so alike, both dark and thin with long sort of bendy limbs. She could imagine them swinging and leaping from bar to bar like trapeze artists, or from tree to tree. She smiled politely when they both turned to her as if asking for approval and admiration of their darling son.

He really isn't a bit like his parents, she thought later, contemplating Leo as he lay in his cot. Mrs Bamber had dithered nervously before leaving as if she doubted Katy's intelligence and ability. It was her husband who eventually put his long hands on her shoulders and gently guided her from the room.

"He doesn't usually wake up. He shouldn't need anything," she had repeated while Katy stood trying to look calm and capable. "Whatever you do, don't let the side of the cot down, will you? He can scramble out and he gets into everything and does a lot of damage if he's loose, um, just playing of course, but he can be a bit of a handful. Well, you won't I know… and he has to be kept warm so don't turn the heating down." She was still muttering warnings as she left the house.

Katy sat in a large cushioned armchair, the cover of which was pulled and torn, as if several cats had tested their claws on it. The bedroom was very warm, almost too hot, and very quiet and peaceful. Toys, old and new, torn and chewed, lay in a heap in a large wooden box. The wall behind the big, green-painted cot was papered with a safari print of tall grasses, green and amber and gold; in the distance odd misshapen trees seemed to waver under a hot tremulous sky. The bars of the cot merged with it and the child, in his tawny yellow sleepsuit and sand-coloured sheets, appeared to be a part of it, as if he belonged, ready-camouflaged, in his own little clearing in that foreign environment.

Birds in their little nests, thought the babysitter dreamily. She thought of the gang of four girls, like fledglings in their bramble nest. Not that Leo was at all like a bird; he was fair and compactly built, chunky in fact, with wide hands and feet curled like paws. He

was a large baby, almost too big for his cot. He was two and a bit years old, she had been told, and she wondered why he didn't have a proper bed. His hair, another shade of yellow, deeper than the sand sheet, fanned around his head making peaks like the petals of a sunflower. His nose was broad and made you want to reach out and pat it; his eyes reflected the green and gold of the colour scheme. All in all she considered that he looked like a big cuddly cub.

She stirred lazily; it was getting much too hot, uncomfortably so. Katy moved to the radiator and turned it off, making a mental note to switch it back on as soon as the temperature had fallen sufficiently. She yawned and smiled sleepily at the child who lay, eyes open a crack, with a patient, time-biding smile as if he was purring.

"Whaa...?" It was a noise which had woken her and for a few seconds she wondered where she was. It seemed that she was, incredibly, at a zoo. There were bars in front of her, dark stripes, ominous in the dim light and cool air: bars outlined against other shadowy vertical shapes, all merging in a menacing manner as if gathering together, advancing towards her, attacking. She stared in disbelief while memory returned; the wallpaper, the cot... where was the baby? The sound which had woken and alarmed her dozy mind came again. It was loud, threatening. Her ears seemed to shrivel on her head.

"Grrr, grrr, grroarrr," a full-throated roar split her muddled thoughts and splintered the atmosphere, leaving only fear filling her mind and spreading through her body so that her limbs jerked with shock and would not be stilled. Something had sprung up behind the bars, something menacing, dangerous. There, on all fours, pacing back and forth, wrathful, powerpacked, terrifying, was a lion.

The fearful sight caused Katy to press against the back of the armchair, her heels digging into the edge of the seat and sticking there. The whole thing was unreal, a nightmare; it just could not be happening, not for real. The small light, which had been left on a shelf by the cot, caused shadows to leap and lurk against the grassy background, caught the flash of eyes like beams of danger, and made the prowling figure immensely huge and terrifying.

As she watched, the animal reared up, gripping the wooden bars awkwardly with its forepaws. The rattle

and scratch of its claws was alarming but worse followed instantly; the bars began to shake. Now the rattling was the side of the cot jerking against the metal catches and there was nothing awkward about the strength and determination which rocked the flimsy wooden structure. How long would the catches hold against such fury?

Katy slid a foot towards the floor, preparing to make a dash for the door. The shaking intensified as if her movement had excited the creature. Horrified, she saw the catches swing upwards and the side of the cot slam down. She turned back, and in one movement, she climbed onto the arm and from there onto the back of the big, old chair. Then she was slithering down behind it, thankful that it was in a corner.

As she slid headfirst to the floor she heard, but did not see, the soft padding feet crossing the room. She felt the thud as the beast landed heavily on the seat of the armchair. Terror invaded her as the denim cloth of her jeans was gripped and torn, and her right ankle grazed, by claws snatching at her fast-disappearing foot. The impetus of the animal's landing and her own jerking progress had pushed the chair as far back as it would go and she crouched behind it sobbing, like a small hunted thing in its bolthole, grateful that the chair was solid right down to the ground.

The growling was very near and, added to it, were little thumps which she realised were made by the animal jumping playfully up and down, trying to leap over the back of the high chair. She imagined it descending, landing on top of her, claws extended and sharp teeth bared. It was a few minutes before she realised that the moaning noise she could hear was being made by herself.

Now there were different noises, like a puppy worrying a slipper, sounds of tearing threads. She shifted to ease an ache in her right ankle and her left foot slipped from cover. Instantly a paw reached down and batted the sole of her trainer; the cub tumbled down with joyous yelps and scrabbled at the carpet where her foot had been. It was playing a game with her – a game which it was enjoying!

How had it all come about? She whimpered and shivered in her den, crouched with her arms about her knees, her head tucked down. The baby, that small boy, had become this dangerous wild thing – this monster. There was no doubt about it. He looked almost the same but short golden fur, like velvet, grew on his body, his hands had become sharp wounding weapons, and his teeth… she shuddered.

He was like something out of a horror film – a werelion. She almost giggled aloud at the thought but instead swallowed hard to quell her hysteria. The lion cub was quiet. What was it doing? She dared not move and she was getting very stiff. Was that a clawing, tearing sound from the back of the chair? She raised her head cautiously and yelped as she saw the bright eyes, the ruff of sandy hair, the teeth. It was looking down at her, gathering itself to…

A shrill ringing startled the animal and it slipped back, dragging at the upholstery as it went.

Telephone, thought Katy, and fainted.

"Hush," a voice said. "Don't make a sound. Don't want to wake the baby, do we?" Someone was standing over her. She had the sensation of having been moved, lifted bodily, of whisperings surrounding her, of being contained in the thoughts and decisions of others so that she felt, even before she remembered where she was, that everything had already been sorted out. She looked up from the depths of the old armchair into Mr Bamber's dark, smiling face.

"Sorry to have to wake you," he said. "You looked so cosy. Comfortable old chair isn't it?"

She drew back, shuddering. "The lion," she gasped and stared across the room. Mrs Bamber was bending over the side of the cot and tucking a cover gently around a sleeping form. "It's back in the cage."

"What?"

"The... the... the lion... your baby... it's wild, a wild animal... it turned into a lion and tried... tried... tried..." She burst into tears in which fear, perplexity and relief all had some part.

"My dear girl, what on earth are you talking about? Did you have a nightmare? Is that what...? Ssshh, you'll wake him, he's sleeping beautifully."

She snuffled into a tissue which was put into her hand, aware of adult disapproval and ashamed, in spite of herself, to be making a fuss.

"He... rattled the bars till the catch gave way and then..." she tried again. "He clawed my leg... look..." she showed the tear at the edge of her jeans and relived the moment with an attack of hiccups.

"You have been having a bad dream, haven't you? Do you often have nightmares?" The voice was subdued, sympathetic but also critical. "I didn't realise you were so, well, imaginative."

Clearly it was not a good thing to be. She was not a sensible, reliable person after all. Was that a quick glance exchanged between husband and wife? Had they planned what they would say to her, how they would make it all seem like her imagination, make her feel that she was behaving in a ridiculous manner? Could it have been a dream? She stood up and gazed at the figure in the cot while Mrs Bamber, with a simpering smile, stood to one side to allow her to do so.

The small face was now pink, the broad curling fingers lay outside the sheet, the golden hair had been smoothed down. She wiped her forehead with the

edge of her sleeve. It was damp, she was unbearably hot. Could she be ill?

"Look," she said, and lifted her foot to show the scratches, the ripped cloth, presenting the only piece of evidence she had, for the baby was a baby again, no doubt of that.

"There must be a nail sticking out of that old chair," the man frowned. "Sorry about that. I'll have a look for it, can't have Leo getting caught on it." He began to move around the chair, stooping and breathing hard as he felt around the edges. The room was so hot that perspiration showed in beads on his face.

"Ah, yes, here it is." He jerked hard, pulling at something. "One of those upholstery pins – nasty thing, could be dangerous." Katy stared and suddenly, unexpectedly, fury welled up in her. She would not put up with this. She knew what had happened.

"I tell you he's dangerous," she yelled, while they made shushing noises at her. "He turned into a lion, he attacked me…" Her voice trailed away as she realised the impossibility of it all. The man began to shake with silent laughter, bony shoulders moving up and down, arms lightly swinging.

"We're going to have to change that wallpaper," he told his wife. "If it has this effect on a babysitter, well," he took out a handkerchief and wiped his face, "it could give him nightmares too, when he's a bit older."

"It wasn't a dream, I keep telling you, it was real…" Was it? She felt tired, fed up with the whole thing.

She tried once more, but without conviction, "He

escaped from his cage."

They both turned shocked faces to her and hustled her towards the door. In spite of everything, she allowed herself to be manoeuvred.

On the landing Mr Bamber took her firmly by one arm.

"Now look here," he gave her a little cross shake before letting go. "I'm sorry you had a bad dream and tore your jeans but I will not put up with this any longer. My child does not, repeat not, sleep in a cage. He is a perfectly normal little boy and you are behaving like a silly, hysterical girl who is trying to draw attention to herself with wild tales. This nonsense must stop, do you hear?" He sounded very angry, in a perfectly normal sort of way, like any father – like her father.

She saw how foolish her story sounded. Nobody could believe in it, certainly not her own parents.

"Well," said Penny. "Did they have a ghastly secret? Did you find any evidence?"

It was two days later and the memory of that evening did now seem like a bad dream. Katy felt embarrassed whenever she thought of it.

"Oh, they're just a bit odd, that's all. A bit like animals," it came out before she could stop it. She blushed. "Some people are," she finished.

"What do you mean?" Francie demanded. "They eat like pigs?" She snorted loudly, "Or smell like skunks?" She made a rude noise and everyone giggled, except Katy.

"Well, her experience of babysitting doesn't seem to have been encouraging exactly. She was a bit odd, withdrawn, when she came home that evening." Katy's mother was speaking on the phone to her sister. "Yes, it's a shame but she's very anti-baby at the moment so you'd better leave asking her for a bit. She swore she wouldn't babysit ever again. What? Oh, just the people next door. They seem a nice young couple, very quiet, you know. Yes, just the one child. He seems quite a bright little thing, very destructive though, judging by the things that get thrown out, but there you are, children just don't know how to look after things these days; they have so much. No, I haven't spoken to them but he told Jack he's a scientist doing research of some kind. What's that? No, no I – don't think he's that sort, no, he works with animals I believe… something experimental."

Waiting to be Collected

"Stop it, you'll pull my arm off!" I screeched, flinging myself backwards. My sister turned, gave a vicious jerk and pulled again. Her mouth had gone all thin and stiff and her cheeks were a bad-tempered red.

"Right, that's it!" she declared. "You can walk home on your own. I've had enough. I'm not stopping again whatever happens. Mooning about and wasting time when it will soon be dark. I'm off and you'd better keep up if you don't want to get lost."

She let go of my hand and I looked at the red marks her fingers had made. She was walking away fast and already she had got as far as the bend in the road.

"Wait for me!" I yelled. A little sob of self pity rose in me and I let it out in a kind of hiccup. My feet were aching, poor soles (ha, ha), and they flapped reluctantly along the pavement like a pair of orphaned flippers.

It was not, repeat not, my fault that we had missed the bus. After all, I was the one who was ready in time and I could have caught it, but my sister was busy talking to some boy she knew and although I called out, she took no notice until it was too late. She ran then, but it was too late by far. The driver seemed to think it was a race and put on speed.

"I told you," I said. She was furious – *with me!* How unfair can you get? All sisters seem to get like that when they hit thirteen or fourteen, I've noticed that. I've seen other people's sisters go the same way. They get all bossy and unbearable. You must have seen the way they stand in giggly groups all over the place and flutter their eyelashes and look sideways at boys. I shan't get like that. I mean, it's not compulsory, is it?

"We'll walk," she'd said, and that was that.

She was still ahead of me when I rounded the bend, so I slowed down. I wasn't going to rush after her. She was to blame after all, not me. My feet were aching a lot and when I stopped they got worse, and one of my big toes felt all squashed as if someone was standing on it. It was all her fault. Why couldn't we have waited for the next bus, that's what I wanted to know. She said walking would be quicker, but I hadn't agreed, had I? I wasn't asked, was I? I suppose I'm not a person any more to her, just a kind of parcel to be lugged around. She ought to carry me. I almost laughed out loud thinking about it. I'm nearly as big as she is though I'm four years younger.

She was crossing the road now and turning down an alley that led from one road to another – it turned at a right angle and saved you having to go all around the corner. I saw her glance back before she crossed, to make sure that I was following. Now she was swallowed up by the dim alleyway, like being gulped down a throat. What if she never came out at the other end? No such luck.

When I reached the entrance to the alley, she was nearly at the end of the passage. It was darker here because of the garden walls, all fairly high in the narrow passageway. There were trees too, overhanging in places and gloomy with dusk. It was very quiet, shut away from the traffic. There was a light halfway along and it shone on a big plastic dustbin, black and dusty. I went as far as the bin and crouched down behind it. I didn't want Liz to see me. I wasn't going to follow her. After all, I could get home very well on my own; I didn't have to stay with her. I mean, it's not compulsory, is it?

After a few seconds, though, she came back to look for me. I could hear her steps coming slowly and as softly as she could tread; she knew I was hiding. When she'd looked along the length of the alleyway, she gave up trying to keep quiet.

She called out, "Josie?" and I pressed back against the fence, trying to make myself invisible. The fence gave slightly and I felt a gap. I pushed on backwards through the gap, and suddenly I was in a shadowy corner of a garden. She'd never find me now and it would serve her right.

She'd have to give up looking soon and go home on her own. Then she'd really be in trouble because, although I'm ten and quite capable of looking after myself, well, you know what parents are like, she was supposed to be looking after me (what a joke). I held my breath and waited.

There was smoke drifting across from somewhere and I could smell burning. Some bonfire! The smell was awful and the smoke was thick and black. There was clogging, suffocating dust in the air and bits of soft black stuff, like dark snowflakes, that settled and clung to me. I could feel it in my nose and throat, choking me and making me cough. My eyes were stinging and I put an arm up over them, as I stumbled further into the garden. Flakes of grey ash drifted in the thinner air as I left the murkiness behind.

I took from my pocket the wad of tissues, which I'd pinched from the box Liz keeps by her bedside, wet one with spit and tried to rub my eyes clear. I had a go at rubbing the marks on my denim jacket but they just sank into the cloth, so I gave up.

It was still pretty dark, even away from the smoke, but all the same I wondered if I was being watched – just a feeling I had. I expected someone to rap on a window and shout at me. I peered into the gloom... I wasn't in a garden after all.

I was definitely standing on a patch of grass, though, weedy green with patches of that sour-smelling stuff with tiny yellow flowers. There was a road with houses on the far side – at least, one house stood out clearly and there seemed to be others, but they were kind of shadowy, as if night had come to them already.

In front of the house was a low brick wall with metal stumps sticking out of the top of it, as if railings had been chopped off. There was a gateway too, without a gate. A short flight of stone steps led up to a porch and, sitting on the steps, was a girl of about my own age.

I suddenly had a brainwave – if I could find my way from here, I might get home before Liz and she'd still be looking for me and tearing her hair out wondering where I was. I looked up and down the road. There was nothing and no-one about, only the girl. It was very still, like it is after a very big noise. It was as if everything had stopped and was waiting, sort of holding its breath. I've noticed before that it can be like that at dusk, as if there's a pause in time, when day has finished and night has not begun.

I crossed the road and stood by the gateway.

"Hi!" I said, grinning at the girl. She looked at me

in a surprised way.

"Are you an American?" she asked.

Now I was surprised, "No."

"Oh." A pause, then she asked, "Are you waiting to be collected, like me?"

"I'll be collected, all right, if my sister gets here. I don't want her to find me, she'll only boss me about."

"As you're here, you might as well sit down and wait, like me."

"No thanks. It's not compulsory, is it?"

She laughed at that. She laughed a lot and I laughed too, a bit, just to be friendly, you know.

"I like your dress," I told her. It was really pretty, though a bit little-girlish. It was made of some flowery material with puffed-out sleeves trimmed with blue, and it had a belt which came from either side of a flat blue piece at her waist and went around her back where I guessed it would be tied in a bow – like I said, a bit kiddyish. She had a cord across one shoulder and I thought it probably was attached to a purse made of the same stuff as her dresss. Not my style; I like jeans best but, as my mum says, we can't all be the same, and after all, it's not compulsory. Anyway, I was trying to be as polite as she was.

"Thank you," she said, looking pleased and smoothing the skirt to her knees.

"Yeah, it's dead fashionable," I went on. For some reason she seemed shocked. "So are the ankle socks," I added.

Well, I would have said she went as white as a sheet, but it wasn't really white, more a sort of fading, as if she was less solid.

"I have to wait here to be collected," she said again.

"Look, can you tell me where this road goes?" I thought I'd better get away if I was going to beat Liz home.

"Nowhere," she replied, and again she seemed alarmed, as if I was asking things that were dangerous or forbidden. "There's nowhere left – only here. I have to wait to…"

"Be collected," I finished for her. I began to think her needle had got stuck in a groove and that was all she could say.

"What is all this about being collected anyway?" I asked.

She just looked at me.

"What's this road called?" I tried. I thought she must know that.

"Balmoral Drive," she replied. "That's what it was."

I decided to overlook that last bit. I was beginning to get a bit edgy. I thought she might be a bit, you know – crackers.

"Balmoral Drive. Great!" I repeated enthusiastically. "Well, what's down that end?" I pointed into the shadows the way I wanted to go.

"Nothing, it's all gone. There's nothing left any more."

I gave up. This girl was potty – a whole two bites short of a snacksize. I walked up the steps and stopped at the side of her.

"Is your mother in?" I asked.

"Oh, I don't live here," she turned her head to me. "I'm just visiting. My mother's coming soon to collect me."

I wished her mother would get here, the sooner the better as far as I was concerned. She was a total dead loss. I went into the porch. There were coloured tiles on the ground. They were bright and polished. There was no bell, only a door knocker, so I banged it up and down a bit.

"There's no-one there," the girl called back at me. She rested her elbows on her knees, then held her chin on her hands and stared into the quiet roadway – waiting.

Stepping back from the porch, I peered at the windows on either side and saw that there was blackness beyond them, like thick black curtains. For some reason, looking at those windows made my insides feel all funny, as if I'd suddenly gone down in a lift. When I looked at the actual glass I could see that it was criss-crossed all over with strips of brown sticky paper, the type that you sometimes see on parcels. The strange weak feeling in my stomach got worse and the hairs on the back of my neck felt as if they were going to lift off. That sticky tape reminded me of something – I wasn't sure what, but I knew that it shouldn't be there, not now, not in my time.

Something very odd was going on and I had the feeling it was going to get odder. I knew now what was wrong with my stomach – fear. I was scared all right. I wished I was somewhere else. I wished I'd gone with Liz. I didn't want to have to turn around and look at that girl again. I was afraid of what I might see, what I might find out. I had to do it though, there was no other way. I made my feet move and turn, so that I could look at her – whatever she might be.

She was still sitting there, still resting her chin on her hands, still staring at the road. Then I saw with a sick dread that the cord over her shoulder supported not a purse but a box, a square, brown cardboard box. Now I knew.

I had seen boxes like that before; I had seen children, and adults too, with those plain brown boxes. I had seen them in old photographs of evacuees and films about World War Two and I knew what was inside that box – a gas mask. A coldness sank right through me, as if my veins were being drained.

Where was I? How had I come to be here, out of time? I had to get away, find my way back somehow. I had to walk past her, down those steps and away.

Walk? Did I say walk? I wanted to run faster than I've ever run in my life, but I knew I wouldn't be able to. It would be like in a nightmare, with me running and running and not getting anywhere, and afraid that at any moment a hand would reach out and grab me from behind.

No, the only thing to do was to walk calmly, the way I'd got here. As I stood there, trying to will my feet to walk and take me with them, she moved and spoke.

"They're all down there, if you want them." She pointed and I looked. There on the right was a huge, grassy mound in the garden. It reminded me of a grave I'd seen in a cemetery soon after a funeral, the earth heaped up over it, only this was much, much bigger.

"What is it?" I croaked from my rusty throat.

"It's the shelter, silly."

"What shelter?" I considered this. "You mean a nuclear fallout shelter?" I was really puzzled.

She laughed out loud. "A what? What are you talking about? The air-raid shelter, of course. You must have one. Is yours an indoor one?"

I just stared at her.

"Listen," she said, "they're singing down there – 'Roll Out the Barrel'. Can you hear?"

I listened. "I can't hear anything."

She frowned. "You are a funny boy," she said.

Boy! I forgot for a moment to be afraid. That really shook me. I mean like I was a tambourine.

She had called me a boy! I moved down two steps from her and was just about to let her have my view on girls begin allowed to wear trousers and have short hair, etcetera, when she stared into the sky and began speaking again.

"It'll be coming in a minute," she cried. "It's nearly time."

A cold hand seized my heart. "Time? What for?" I was looking up too. There was a sort of buzzing sound far off, like a big mechanical insect that was humming its way nearer and nearer.

"My mother's not here yet. She's supposed to collect me." Her anguished voice rang out into the still evening, silent but for that relentless drone.

"Why aren't you in the shelter with the others?" I asked, but I knew the answer. I knew why she sat here and why she had sat on that step all those years ago, just as I knew what must have happened to her. I still wanted to run away but something held me there with her. I couldn't just leave her.

"The all-clear went," she was talking again, explaining in a faraway voice. "It went, you see, so I came out to wait on the steps. They told me not to, they said it wasn't safe yet, that I should wait a bit longer, but I was afraid I'd miss her. She was supposed to come and take me home."

She stood up and looked yearningly towards the road along which nobody came. I joined her on the step and held her hand. She didn't notice, I don't think she knew I was there any more.

"Come on," I said and tugged at her, "we'll both have to run for it."

I knew it was silly even as I said it but I had to try and get her away, away from the awful thing that was going to happen, that I knew had already happened, all those years ago.

The droning stopped. There was silence.

"Doodlebug," she murmured softly. "The noise stops just before they fall."

"Josie," a thin voice was calling from far away.

"Josie," nearer now. Was it Liz? It had seemed to come from the opposite side of the road where the shadows were deepest, the way I had come. I started to run, down the steps, towards the cry, but the strange girl overtook me and went flying through the gateway ahead of me.

"It's her! She's come for me. Now I can go, I can go home…" she was sobbing but there was joy in her voice.

Before she reached the other side she half-turned. "Come on," she cried to me and then… she disappeared.

I was right there behind her and she vanished completely, just as I was pitched forward onto my knees by a great force. I was choking, trying to draw breath and my lungs seemed full of powdered brick and smoke and ash.

"There you are," a voice announced crossly. A hand hauled me upright and started brushing me down.

"Was that you calling me, just now?" I had to know.

"I have been looking for you. I suppose you think it's funny to hide behind dustbins and get yourself covered in muck. It's about time you grew up a bit."

"Liz," I appealed to her, "I… I'm so glad that… that you found me… you don't know what happened, but… I must know, please, did you call my name just now?"

I must have looked as frantic as I felt because she stared and then said, "No. No I didn't. Why do you want to know? I was keeping quiet, actually. I guessed you'd be hiding."

"Thank goodness," I beamed at her. "It's all right then. It really was her mother."

"Whose mother? What do you mean? What's been happening? Are you all right?" She held me at arm's length and studied my face. "You do look a bit odd, now I come to look at you. Are you feeling all right? What's been going on?"

"I went through that gap and I…" I started. I looked at the gap. It was all of six centimetres wide and there were rose bushes behind it, tangled and thorny, trying to push the fence down. There was smoke, though, a thin trail of it drifting, smelling of burning wood. I could hardly think straight.

"There's a house on fire back there," I began. "A bomb, well, a missile of some sort…"

"It's a bonfire, stupid. Trust you to get ash all over you. Look at your jacket. I don't know what Mum will…" I stopped listening.

I let her lead me home, I just tagged along. I tried to keep my mind still, not let it think. I blotted out all that had happened to me and just walked, as if I was a zombie. To give Liz her due, she did seem to be worried about me.

I was shaking all over when I reached home and I couldn't stop it. Mum took my temperature, then rushed me to bed and said I had flu.

When I felt normal again it was like a dream, that house and that girl, as if I'd imagined it. That's what I tell myself when I get frightened thinking about it – that I imagined the whole thing. It doesn't work. I know it was real, all of it… it really did happen.

Next term, I'm going to do a project on our town during Word War Two and I'm going to talk to some of the old people who remember what happened. I'll go to the big library in town and ask to see old newspapers, too. I'm going to start from the date I saw the girl, June 14th it was, and I'll search through the papers for the fifteenth and sixteenth of each year of the war. I know her name you see. She was called Josie, like me, and I know the name of the road where it happened, so it shouldn't be too difficult to find out about that bomb – doodlebug, she called it – and who was killed when it fell and exploded.

When I know her surname, I intend (and this is the scary bit) to check the papers for *this year* and find out if her mother died on June 14th or round about that date.

You see, her mother did come in the end. She did come to collect Josie – I heard her.

Then, when I've done all that research, and I'm sure of what happened, I'll try and forget it. I'll try.

I've never told anyone about this before, about what happened that afternoon, because I doubt if they would believe me and they might try to reason it away. Adults would, I know. They like to tell us that things like that don't happen. To me it makes sense, and that's the way I want it. It is a happy ending after all.

You can believe it or not, I don't mind. After all, it's not compulsory.

Badger

"Oh, bother," the child hesitated, peered through the gap so that pale green leaves framed her flushed face making it smaller and neater. The bonnet she wore was hardly seen but the dark brown curls swung forward with her movement and her long, grey skirt swayed below the branches, showing buckled shoes and dark, rusty coloured stockings.

The woman, who was sitting on a low canvas stool in the churchyard, gasped and rocked precariously. Was that a child staring at her?

"Oh my goodness." Miss Percival's breath seemed in short supply and she put a hand to her throat as if to ease the problem.

"Oh, oh, dear me!" She half stood and the large drawing pad, which had rested on her broad lap, slithered to the gritty path. The light-weight seat, no longer pinned to the earth by her bulk, rocked and tipped backwards. It increased her alarm. She felt surrounded, that strange things were happening in every direction, triggered by some coincidence of time and place. Resting a hand on the cool marble of the monument she had been drawing, she wondered if the sudden weakness meant that she was about to faint, an experience which would be new to her, or whether she could control her muscles sufficiently well to scream or shout and attract attention.

There was a scuffle in the dried leaves, a tremor of twigs and a diminishing giggle. The apparition disappeared from sight.

Miss Percival, leaning on the unresponsive stone, wondered if she had seen a ghost or had imagined that small figure. She picked up her belongings, righted the stool and looked with dismay at the lettering she had been copying from the Anstruther family tomb:

> Elizabeth Charlotte Anstruther
> died 1813, aged ten years

That was the reason for it, no doubt. It must be that her mind had formed a picture as she worked, and had projected it into the near distance when she looked up, so that the imagined child had appeared before her. The very fact that she had seen so little – a hint of a face, bonnet, skirt – strengthened this theory. She was tired and fatigue could play strange tricks.

She was well aware of this; sometimes when she was alone at night, asleep or half-asleep in her special armchair, she heard voices. They were quite clear – snatches of sentences, exclamations, familiar voices of people that she had known long ago. Often they called her name but she always knew that they were in her head, that her brain, like a tape recorder, was playing back to her these almost forgotten sounds. There was something almost quite comforting about it in a way. Her mother's voice was recalled speaking to her as if she was a child again.

Seeing things was different though. It was surely much more serious. For a moment a little speck of anxiety caught at her but she suppressed it; squashed it flat.

"Nonsense," she said out loud. Here she was in the open air, on a sunny day in May. There were people within reach, not far away, and she had a job to do. In fact she hadn't all that much time left to finish the job. She had been slowing down, daydreaming. She plonked herself on the sagging canvas in a hearty no-nonsense manner and applied herself to her task. This church must be finished today or she would be behind with the whole project. No more imaginings, she told herself and, planting her feet as if she meant to leave their imprint deep in the soil, she rummaged in her large squashy leather bag until she located a packet of biscuits. A few were released into the depths as she fumbled one free from the wrappings; crumbs dropped down the front of her bulky jacket. A large black cat with one white streak across its head strolled past elaborately ignoring her.

Miss Percival sighed and felt satisfactorily normal again. She always felt better after a biccy.

"Er... I didn't expect to find you still here, Miss Percival. Lucky you didn't get locked in for the night, eh?" The vicar laughed to show there was really no cause for fearing that such a thing was probable, and also because he found the woman's gaze disconcerting. She had a habit of staring, as if she expected to find the answers to unasked questions written upon his face. There was a pause before she spoke and, when she did, her voice surprised him once again with its high girlish tones, as if a child still lived in the bulging body with it's wiry grey hair.

"Mr Dowser," she began, "I had a most extra-ord-inary..." she strung out the word as if it was one she had just learned and was trying out for the first time. "Really a most extraordinary experience in the churchyard this afternoon." Wonderingly, with eyes fixed on his face, she told of the child she had seen gazing from the shelter of the trees. The vicar was relieved. If that was all that was bothering her, then he did have an explanation.

"I see, and you thought... My dear Miss Percival, I'm so sorry if you were upset. The fact is that the children were rehearsing – a pageant, historical you know. We are holding it on the first of July, part of our annual fete. It's rather special this year, our three hundred and fiftieth. I imagine it was one of our choirgirls you saw. I do hope..."

He laughed a little, not too much, and apologised, thinking that the old dear might have had a nasty shock. "I hope you were not too discomposed. Really, it's quite a compliment to our wardrobe mistress that you should think... but I can quite see that it might have been a little worrying."

Again the wait before she spoke. "Ah, I always believe that there must be a rational explanation for everything. I assure you that I do not believe in ghosts. I don't want you thinking me a silly old biddy who jumps to conclusions."

"Of course not."

"Well, since there are no ghosts here, perhaps I might be allowed to stay a little while longer and complete my work on the inside of the building. I really ought to finish here today. I have to move on to Little Harlock on Monday and time is short. I shall only be," she looked around, "about an hour more, an hour and a half at the very most."

"Ah." The clergyman was uneasy. He pursed his lips and jingled his keys in his cassock pocket.

"There can be no harm, surely?"

"Er, no, of course not, no harm. That is... there is nothing here that could harm you, of course not. Nothing to cause you any concern. If you would just bolt the door after me now – to make sure there are no intruders -- then I will return in just over an hour to lock up after you have finished."

Miss Percival worked her way around the church, the lights shining on black marble and gold lettering, on stone figures unrelaxed upon their tombs, on a row of gilded infants, kneeling in order of age on a Jacobean memorial; their names and short lives recorded with those of their parents.

A tiny sound, like fingers moving against something hard, crept into her concentration. Scratch, scratch. There it was again. She frowned and looked up from her work. Scratch, scratch. It was a delicate sound as of little fingernails working on an unyielding surface and it seemed to be coming from the top of the large coffin-shaped stone monument. The stained glass window high above could only be seen as a mixture of light and darkness now that daylight no longer shone upon it; in one corner of it, low down, something moved.

Scratch, tap, tap – a tapping on the glass. Thorny fingers trying to gain entrance. Twigs, just twigs, the dead and dried limbs of a climbing rose that still clung to the earth and leaned against the church wall as if seeking admittance.

Miss Percival was not frightened. Since learning of her mistake that afternoon she had grown courageous. Everything has a rational explanation. She believed that, because, of course, it was true. She had proved it that very day, not once, but twice. She continued with her work.

A tiny noise, very different from the scratching of the thorns, was whispered on the still air as if to test her nerve. A mewing, small and faint, like an infant's cry, a rustle of things shifting and stirring, moving on the cold draught which swept across the tiled floor and swirled around her feet. She was hearing things again. It was simply tiredness she knew that – better concentrate and get finished. Her hands were becoming stiff. She made a mistake and had to rewrite a name: Samuel Joseph Farlling, died 1763, aged two years.

A patter of small feet sounded nearby. There was no mistaking it. Her neck seemed to grow stiff and a cold shiver ran along her spine. Tiny feet pattering on wood, coming along the raised floor from behind the great family tomb. This could not be happening.

She stepped back and came up against the high back of a pew. Pencil and pad fell to the floor unregarded. There was movement, quite definitely movement; something was happening. Something, or someone, other than herself, was here in this echoing building and it was approaching. Her mouth was dry. She pressed harder against the wood of the pew as if she hoped to enter it. The pattering was louder, round from the back of the huge carved bulk of the stone it came. It was a small creature, she knew, she could tell. She closed her eyes and held her shaking body upright by gripping fiercely the polished wood.

There was a moment when she knew she was being regarded, a moment of silence. Something was very close to her, she could sense it; there was a feeling of being looked at by a curious, but friendly, being. Her eyes opened, no longer being able to bear the not-knowing.

The black cat with the white stripe narrowed its golden eyes at her. A scrunched paper lay near its forepaws. Withdrawing its attention from her, the cat crouched and swung the rear of its body from side to side, thrashing the long black tail on the dusty floor. It sprang, caught the paper and tossed it capriciously away, then batted the plaything so that it skitted along the central aisle.

Miss Percival drew in great gulps of air. "There is always a rational explanation for everything," she told the building, and the words followed the cat up the brilliantly lit nave and fell more softly in the shadowy corners of the church.

"It was after all, nothing to worry about, very foolish of me, so silly."

"Not at all. It would scare anyone." The vicar's wife filled her guest's coffee cup for the third time. "Those tombs are a little overwhelming, I often think." She wondered if Miss Percival would be gone before her favourite Saturday evening serial began on television.

"I was nervous, can't blame the cat."

"The cat! So you saw Badger, did you? He's very naughty, I'm afraid, keeps coming into the church."

"Well, there is, after all, a rational explanation for everything. That's what I always say." The coffee cup was drained and Miss Percival collected her belongings together.

The vicar locked the church door with the long, heavy, iron key and walked through the graveyard, shining his torch ahead of him along the path of pale stones. Near the gate he stopped and, moving onto mossy grass, stooped down and touched the curved head of a cat. "Up to your old tricks, eh, Badger?" He patted it. "You'll have to learn to choose your times better, old friend."

He stood again and the torchlight slid over the shape of a crouching cat, carved in stone. A small metal plate set in the earth was briefly lighted:

In Memory of Badger,
the church cat, 1976 - 1990.